I0760415

PRAISE FOR
SONGS FROM FERN'S POND

"A stirring poetic tribute. . . . Quick bursts of natural descriptions result in powerful moments . . . evok[ing] the careful attentiveness of famed ecologists, with nature made to mingle with human dramas throughout. Blending elements of memorialization with nature writing, *Songs from Fern's Pond* is a poetry collection that explores loss, family, and the power of human will." —*Foreword* Clarion Reviews

"A beautifully impressionistic weaving of anecdotes, poetry, and personal letters and an ode to the seasons of a year, of a life, and of a lineage. Harmer has created, in her mother, Fern, a richly unforgettable protagonist and matriarch. As the weaving continues, much like with her own baskets, the warp and weft of Fern's life becomes ever more discernible. And readers will find, in the end, that it is the interspersal of the rough and the smooth, the ordinary and the bold, that makes the finished product one of such unique and memorable beauty. If what they say is true—that life is a work of art and we must all endeavor to remain its artist—we could do worse than follow in the path of Fern, who met the rough and the smooth with good cheer and never ceased living her life with generosity and intention." —Alexandra A. Chan, author of *In the Garden Behind the Moon*

"How privileged we are to see a life through another's eyes . . . a life we would have never known, never crossed paths with if not for Sheryl Pothier Harmer's *Songs from Fern's Pond*. In this collection, Harmer intersperses poems depicting the life of Fern—a hard-working woman full of love and grit—with actual letters the author and family received from Fern throughout her life. Some are very slice-of-life, and some will make you chuckle, but they all tell a story. Harmer illustrates beautifully through these poems and letters how the seasons of our life change, how the world as we know it is here for a time then gone, how it takes every single moment to truly live a life. *Songs from Fern's Pond* so eloquently takes us out of our own lives and puts us into hers. It's sure to leave a legacy on the hearts of readers for years to come, which, I feel confident, is how Fern would have intended." —Amber Showalter, poet and author of *Death Will Be Our Curfew*

"*Songs from Fern's Pond* contains the essence of not just surviving, but thriving. Herein lie the keys to adaptation, positivity, and joy that readers can easily learn from. A memoir, an artist's journey, a celebration of nature, a learning opportunity that supports ongoing life education, or an uplifting story of adaptation and joy . . . highly recommended." —Midwest Book Review

Songs *from* Fern's Pond

Songs *from* Fern's Pond

Composing a Life with Courage, Gratitude, and Joy

SHERYL POTHIER HARMER

GFB

fernspond.com

Quotes on pages v and 1 from *Composing a Life* by Mary Catherine Bateson (Grove Press, 1989).

Published by GFB™, Seattle
www.girlfridayproductions.com

Produced by Girl Friday Productions

Cover design: Megan Katsanevakis
Development & editorial: Abi Pollokoff
Production editorial: Kylee Hayes
Project management: Emilie Sandoz-Voyer

Image credits: Front cover photograph courtesy of the author. Back cover © Shutterstock/Lisla. Interior images © Shutterstock/jacobhenry7055; Shutterstock/Natata; Shutterstock/surassawadee

ISBN (hardcover): 978-1-964721-39-2
ISBN (paperback): 978-1-959411-15-4
ISBN (ebook): 978-1-964721-40-8

Library of Congress Control Number: 2024927342

First edition

Fern Rosenlof Pothier. Basket maker. (1984)

Women today, trying to compose lives . . . do not have an easy task.

—Mary Catherine Bateson, *Composing a Life*

Undulating memories,
hazed by the veil of time,
weave their broken shadows
across my lonely mind. . . .
Sheryl Pothier Harmer

DEDICATION

For Fern's sixteen grandchildren.
Some she knew—some she didn't. But she loved them all.

CONTENTS

Fern's Pond: 1976–1989

Summer and Fall

Winter and Spring

PROLOGUE

How do women compose a life that will, as Mary Catherine Bateson put it, "honor all their commitments and still express all their potential with a certain unitary grace"?

Her name was Fern and she was my mother.

I think she was a remarkable woman. Not remarkable in the sense that she changed the world in a profound way. Remarkable in the resilience with which she creatively composed her authentic life—with integrity to her own values and passions. Fern embraced what was offered in the best way she could and gave back with her whole heart—with *courage, gratitude, and joy in the simple things.*

Fern was born in 1913, at a time when the world around her was mostly poor, living in the dust and the desperation of the early twentieth century. Like most families in her rural Oregon community, hers barely scraped by. But in spite of scarcity and grit, her life was filled with love and laughter—people surviving from day to day and year to year—finding beauty in the wildflowers, grace in the sunsets, optimism in the morning dew.

Fern lived a full life—starting with the simplicity and hardship of her small-town origins, navigating the deep national Depression, finding her own footing by putting herself through nursing school, enduring a world war, and becoming a full partner to Oscar. She was by his side during their thirty-three-year marriage—as nurse and cook in his mining camps to supportive executive wife. Together, Fern and Oscar raised four children: my two sisters, our brother, and me.

After Oscar's sudden death when they were both sixty-one, she began to create her final chapter. She sold the family home, found a new community, and with a determination guided by her passions, she established the home of her dreams on Fern's Pond.

Fern was an artist and a weaver. She was a painter and a maker of stained glass doors. Most of all, she created one-of-a-kind baskets from materials she harvested from her land, baskets she exhibited and sold and gave away as treasured gifts. Her imagination and creativity and curiosity were endless. And, in the same way, her life itself became a rich tapestry woven from the bits and pieces of daily life—often messy, always interesting, colorful, and textured.

Fern was a gardener and a nurturer—of plants and animals and humans. The cultivation of a bounty of vegetables and fruits, as well as a vineyard full of grapes, filled her summers; the fall harvests filled her table. And she joyfully gifted her produce, fresh eggs, and homemade breads and pies to neighbors and passersby. With unwavering devotion, she tended her sheep, chickens, calf, and her beloved dog, Rowdy. The mallard ducks that lived on the pond came to her every morning for their breakfast.

She was also a community builder and loved to entertain. Her energy led efforts to create a town historical society and establish a regional arts festival. Her home hosted gatherings such as style shows, dances, and wine-tasting events—complete with treats served on her cut-glass crystal. Her door was always open. Fern's wit was quick and nonjudgmental; her spontaneous and hearty laugh often brought her to tears (which she always wiped with her "hankie"—one of Oscar's big white handkerchiefs).

Fern loved music. She played the piano for the church choir, having retired her old saxophone and guitar. And always, sometimes quietly within herself and often robustly from her heart, she sang—to her grandkids, her garden, her animals, and to herself—silly ditties, choir favorites, and especially old cowboy songs that told familiar stories from her past.

Fern was also a realist. My mother inspired me to live fully and optimistically. She taught that every life has obstacles and opportunities to see oneself as either a victim or as a participant in creatively navigating a new path. Using a lifetime of problem-solving skills, sheer grit, and good humor, she learned her way through each new challenge.

She wasn't naive about the issues she faced, but she lived each day with fearless acceptance, the most that any of us can aspire to do as we lead our own authentic lives from day to day, from year to year.

Fern was, finally, a writer—with her own unique voice. She wrote the letters in this book to family members and friends over a period of fourteen years. They have been reproduced largely as she wrote them in order to capture her voice, energy, personality, humor, and even sometimes quirky spellings and grammar (e.g., lay vs lie). They reflect her robust spirit and boundless determination. She loved her life. She loved living.

Songs from Fern's Pond is a collage—a composition of my original poetic and prose stories and Fern's letters from her years on Fern's Pond—tracing the arc of the last chapter of my mother's life.

Sheryl Pothier Harmer

Beginning—Again

1976

Fern had spent several days along the Snake River in southern Idaho a few years earlier when she'd taken a pottery class there, learning how to work with the thick clay deposits along the riverbank. After Oscar died and she was ready to rebuild her life, she remembered it fondly when thinking about a place where she would feel safe and protected, where she would be free to explore her own creativity and reinvent herself for the last stage of her life.

"Here, ducky, ducky, . . . come, ducky, ducky." A lone figure on the east high bank overlooking the small pond calls out—arm outstretched, face turned to the morning sky. The woman's a beacon in her red plaid jacket, stocking cap pulled tight over her cropped white hair, Levi's cuffed above high-top tennis shoes. Reaching into the dish towel tied around her waist, she grabs handfuls of rich, golden grain and splays them along the driveway. "Here, ducky, ducky. . . Here, ducky, ducky." She's calling the flock home.

From the far length of the pond, the wild ducks call back, gathering to respond. Rising together, they head home. Time for their breakfast. Fern breathes deeply into the morning breeze, scanning the dawn sky. "Come, ducky, ducky," she insists. The birds spiral overhead, pulling in the strays, then drop down low over the pond and circle toward the house. The draft of wings rattles the fringe of cattail reeds along the shore as the flock settles onto the bank. The green heads and iridescent feathers of the drakes mingle with the brown-flecked hens and soft new coats of the adolescents.

"Well, hellooooo there!" Fern calls. "It's about time you showed up." She cackles. "Come on now; you better nibble this up—I've got to get going. Lots to do today—you kids aren't the only ones who have to eat!" She shuffles among the birds, chattering back to them as they nuzzle the dirt beneath her feet.

These third- and fourth-generation ducks have forgotten their fear of humans. They rely on the woman to supplement their already plentiful food supply. Fern has seen the flock tame and bond with the routine over the years since she found this thumb of land surrounded on three sides by a spring-fed pond and grounded on the east by the massive black lava cliffs.

She was drawn to the valley in the months following Oscar's death, her heart hungering to express her deepest, most real self. She longed for a life that might emerge from her own creative interpretation of her heart's callings: harvesting and reshaping nature's gifts, tilling and gardening the fertile ground, continuing her practice as the oldest continuously registered nurse in the state, nurturing her grandchildren, tending to her neighbors and her soul.

———

Aquifer

An underground reservoir
the size of Lake Erie
lies restless
beneath the moonscape lava flow
that blankets southern Idaho.

Fed with winter's melt
and deep springs
from high alpine meadows,
the subterranean lake
anchors the base of the central mountain
range.

There the water gathers and grows and
descends—

trickling, twisting, tumbling,
carving paths, taking riches, replenishing
life.
A confluence of forces
gathers the source
and delivers it to its destination,

only to disappear underground.

Diving deep, the Lost Rivers pause to rest
in the hidden pool that lies below.
Then, fingers of water feel forward—
blindly seeking light.

Coursing through ancient conduits

and underground veins,
the waters rush.
Gravity pulls; momentum pushes—
rolls, rushes, carves, seeks—
until, at last, reaching the moonscape
    edge—
release.

Waters cold and clear spill
from the Thousand Springs
down six-hundred-foot lava cliffs
and tumble into the lush arms
of the Snake River
where it slices a fertile path
through the dry prairie desert,
creating the Magic Valley.

And some of that water,
pure and life-giving,
wends its way
through secret passages
along the foot of the cliffs
to Fern's Pond.

From between moss-coated rocks,
it gently parts the fringe of
watercress along the bank
and bubbles into daylight.
Free.
Not unlike Fern emerging into a new life.

—

And so, responding to the pull of the valley, in 1976, she packed the old Pontiac with homemade biscuits, cheese, fried chicken, and apples, then drove four hours across the desert from Pocatello, down the steep incline off the freeway, and into the Magic Valley. The small town's three hundred residents clustered loosely around the town center and on farms in the surrounding canyons and flats that framed the high plateau above the Snake River. A city park, high school, two churches, post office, one grocery, a Quik Stop service station, pizza joint, bank, slouching motel, a couple of bars, and a declining hardware store were strewn along the one main street.

Framing her destination, a metal awning was hung over a dusty window filled with flies and fading posters. A peeling sign over the door spelled out "Magic Valley Real Estate." Inside, a middle-aged man lounged behind a metal desk—newspaper open, cheap shoes propped on a footstool nearby. Real estate agent, for sure. He looked the part. Dressed in polyester pants, too-short tie, plaid summer jacket. Short buzz-cut hair, black glasses. *A buttoned-up Mormon type,* she thought. *Oh well, they're usually honest.* "I'm Fern." She stuck out her hand for a vigorous shake. "Wondering if you have any property for sale."

"Any property?" They had plenty of that in this forgotten town. Larry knew every plot along the five streets—nothing much moved around here. He sized her up: Short, cropped white hair, mid-sixties-ish, fit in that square, solid, Scandinavian way. Buttoned blouse under an open man's shirt, sleeves rolled up, knee-length skirt, nylons, red Keds. Impish smile, crinkled eyes.

Little house in town, he guessed to himself. *Close by the grocery store and church. Small yard. Not much upkeep—big enough for a few tomato plants and a mouser cat.* He knew the type.

"Someplace with water," she continued. "Water's important. I want to find a place to build a homestead." He perked up. *Homestead? That certainly could mean more than a small house on a patch of land.* He was trained to spot opportunity. "In town or out?" he asked tentatively.

"Oh, out of town. I need room for a cow and some chickens and maybe a sheep or two. I want a place for a garden and plenty of room to roam around. Five or ten acres ought to do."

Now you're talkin', he thought—but still not sure. "Are you, um . . . will anyone else be . . . er, helping you?"

"Nope. Just me." She looked him square in the eye and chuckled. *Thinks I'm an old lady,* she noted to herself.

"For an old gal, I'm pretty sturdy," she assured him. She smiled at the naive man who was just about to be over his head and clearly underestimating her. Her competitive juices flowing, she decided she should lay it on a little.

"I need room for my sheep wagon and tractor," she casually offered. She watched his eyes widen with surprise. "And, of course, my backhoe," she added, warming to the idea. *Come on, Fernie. Give the kid a break,* the voice inside her whispered. *That might be a little thick. And a slight stretch.* In reality, the tractor was more like a riding lawn mower, and she didn't really have a backhoe. Yet. Of course, the part about the sheep wagon was absolutely true.

"So, what can you show me?" she challenged.

The man cleared his throat, swallowed, pushed his glasses up a bit. He noted again the red shoes. The firm grip. "Well, as a matter of fact . . ."

As they drove over the rutted road along the edge of the pond, she felt her spirits begin to lift. They parked out on the point, getting there by navigating through ragged sagebrush and jagged rocks to the center of the surrounding eight acres. Grasshoppers sprang to life, parting the path as she stepped from the car and into the deep dust. A lizard skittered away under a rock, and the hot summer sun glared down, sucking the last drops of morning dew from the dry grasses. *Perfect.*

They wandered around the acreage for nearly an hour in

the blistering sun, Larry trailing and panting to keep up with Fern as she strode ahead, chattering with glee over the flat home site, the sloping garden site, the glorious pond teeming with life. The land itself was dry as powder, but the abundance was in the spring-fed pond that formed a U around the point. Wild ducks, geese, muskrats, skunks, raccoons, frogs, and rainbow trout filled the pond with the banks bordered by reeds and willows. Plentitude.

She whooped with glee to discover the smaller upper pond and the three bubbling springs that gurgled up from the rocks. She mopped her face with the white handkerchief she always carried with her and plowed on, scrambling over rocks, testing the soil between her fingers, and, finally, arriving at the shaded patch under the willows at the far end.

There, away from the harsh glare, dainty ferns poked their tender heads out of the mud. All this glory and ferns too! Taking off her shoes, she hiked up her skirt and waded, nylons and all, into the stream that gurgled under the road. Grabbing a handful of watercress, she began to harvest her first crop. "Here, take this home for salad," she commanded Larry. "It's good for you." Of course, he did as he was told.

As they pulled out to leave, Fern turned to run her gaze along the east-bounding line of lava cliffs. She spotted an eagle soaring high above the valley in the thin air and noted its stick nest wedged on top of a sheer wall. Following its flight south, she gasped: There she saw her own profile clearly outlined at the far end of the rimrocks.

Promise

Powder puffed into the still air
and grasshoppers fled
with each step
between twisted sagebrush
and black basalt.

Dusted, Fern surveyed
the neglected parcel of land,
eight parched acres
home only for snakes and lizards,
ants and prairie squirrels.

But then, the water. Oh, all that glorious
water—
bubbling up from deep
underground springs—
a constant flow into the pond
that hugged the land
and sheltered ducks and trout,
frogs and butterflies.

And, finally,
stark against the southern sky,
she saw her profile—
a formation of rock reclining
on the eastern edge
six hundred feet above the valley.
Her forehead. Her nose. Her chin.

Eight acres of dreams waiting for her
to stake her claim

to a new life.

I'll take it, she said. *I'll take all of it.*

And so, this was home. It took her about a year to sell her house in southern Idaho, move to the Magic Valley, sketch and design a sturdy log house, find a builder, and construct her home—compact and cozy, yet magnificent. Whole logs twelve to fourteen inches in diameter were stacked twenty feet high, snug against the elements. The heart of the home wrapped around a soaring two-story lava rock fireplace built with rough lichen-dotted stones from the prehistoric volcanic flow that formed the boundaries of the broad valley.

One bedroom to the east, a sunroom to the southwest, and a music room/library to the north added dimension to the central hearth room. Seven gigantic whole pine logs—each two to three feet in diameter—stretched the length of the ceiling above a three-sided balcony. There, tucked under the eaves, visitors and grandchildren would find their beds or stretch out their sleeping bags. Lulled by the sound of the crackling fire as the coals burned down at night, they would awaken to the snap of new logs and the waft of fresh coffee in the mornings. Outside, a log gazebo anchored the point of land to the west and housed a firepit in the center for warmth on cool nights. An old apricot tree guarded the north side and supported a hammock for midday escapes from the oppressive summer heat.

She built fences for her lambs, a chicken house for the big reds and the feisty little banties, and a stable for a calf. Her garden was an acre with corn, lettuce, carrots, gourds, pumpkins, tomatoes, cabbage, cauliflower, parsnips, raspberries, and strawberries. Another acre became a vineyard, 160 vines in ten rows marching down the slope toward the south pond—a merry mix of chardonnays for wine and plump reds for snacking. Weeds and grasses and reeds and willows offered plenty of material for her basketmaking.

And, bordering the south lawn, she parked a sheep wagon. Complete with a canvas Conestoga top, potbellied stove, and bunk inside, the wagon was a replica of the one her sheepherder father had used so many years ago. It stood as a testament to how far she had come from her childhood of deep poverty and hard struggle, and she felt her father's spirit within the space.

Behind all her plans and her constant development of the land was the persistent dream of visits from her four children—three girls and one boy—now grown and living their own lives, just starting to have their own children—her grandchildren. After a lifetime of searching, of responsibility, of working hard and doing right, of squeezing her own life into the open cracks between the lives of others, this was her time, and this was her space.

Humility

Fern was not a particularly religious
woman.
Most days she went about her fruitful life
attending to the path
before her—
not necessarily
concerned with the cosmos,
about the meaning
or the purpose
of it all.

But, sometimes,
in the growing whisper
of dusk,
after the sun had rested
and the stars were still
gathering their glow;
when that whisper was broken
by only the sleepy cooing of the doves,
the muttering of a couple
of ducks discussing their day,
and the fat plop of a trout
having one last snack before
sinking into a bed of moss—

sometimes,
she could feel the day shift
from exhale to a sigh,
and she could sense
with awe
her significant insignificance.

Sometimes,
the humility of being a lonely servant
to the earth
in the grandeur of
the universe
brought her to her knees.

Courage, Gratitude, and Joy

1913–1975

The spirits of Fern's pioneer ancestors lingered in the memories held within her soul.

The world they knew was harsh and unrelenting—yet often full of wonder. She came from folks who worked hard their whole life, asked for little, and gave whatever they had with a generous heart.

Fern was raised to see beauty in the wild and stark open prairies. She felt a kinship to the gentle animals hiding in the shadows and the flocks of sheep tended by her father. For the sheepherders, the hard lines of the day were softened by the melodies of the night—the wind over the prairie, the chirp of crickets, the call of coyotes, the murmur of lambs, the gentle nickering of horses, the sounds of dreaming dogs and snapping fires. Their grit was in her bones; their songs flowed through her veins; and their stories fed her dreams.

Her ancestors' courage and joy and grateful acceptance of their complex yet simple lives fueled her optimism and resilience.

Prairie Song

Long shadows hunch around
the crackling campfire
as dusk descends in a whisper—
softening the rough edges
of another hard day.

Bellies full of trout from the brook and
potatoes fried in the
black cast-iron skillet
over an open fire.
Rough hands and sunburned faces
washed clean enough
to end the day
and begin the night.

Quiet joy and pride in the simplicity of a
hard day won.

Sheep softly bleating—
ewes calling to new lambs,
murmuring their protection
against the cry of distant wolves.
Trusty dog dozing in twitching dreams
beside the glowing embers
as the flames die down with the day.

It's then the old cowboy songs begin—
soothing aches of limb and heart.
Gravelly voices—hoarse from

calling across the dusty sage—
rise together in the familiar lines.

"Red River Valley." "Home on the Range."
    "The Strawberry Roan."
A communion of stories
of lost love, longing, and rough valor
passed across the prairie
from campfire to campfire;
sung low while memories drift.

Dear Ones:

I want to tell you about the "Strawberry Roan" song that I love to sing. I couldn't get the recording to work when I switched the tape over, so will write a follow-up. I quit when I was starting to tell an interesting thing about the song. Ray Clawson came in, and I played the tape for him. He exploded that he knew the man who rode the horse and the guy had a brother who wrote the song on a wall in the old bunkhouse where they all worked. Ray was working at that ranch out on Dry Creek in Elko County, Nevada. He said that Walter Holt rode the horse, Old Strawberry Roan, and his brother, Ralph, wrote the words. This was back in 1912.

A few years later, the song was published, but nobody knew the author. It was just copied off the wall. The guy recognized his work when the song got published, but, of course, he couldn't prove it and didn't get any money for it. Kinda fun to have old Ray give this light about the song's beginning.

Lots of love,

Ma

The Sheep Wagon

Idle under the cherry tree,
the old sheep wagon rests,
rusted wheels and tattered tarp,
wooden frame listing in the tall grass—
full of the discards
of Fern's father's strife,
the bare essentials
left over from a life
forged from hardship
and etched by daily toil.

Sagging, weary, and worn, it waits for
    Fritz to return.

Inside it, dim light seeps
between the wooden slats,
piercing the still air
now laced with spiderwebs
and powdered with dust.

This was his home—

his mouse-gnawed quilt
spread upon the narrow bunk,
his potbellied stove
long ago grown cold,
chipped enamel pan,
cast-iron skillet, unlit lantern
on the scarred and wobbly table.

Fritz—father of Fern,

carver of humble gifts of simple beauty
from spare offerings of nature.

He passed his time
out on the prairie—his flock
grazing nearby—carving hand-sized
    chairs
out of sagebrush and pine
for love-worn dolls;

providing for his family
with the skills he had
and longing for his three little girls,
Fuchsia, Fern, and Ellen,
who waited for him in town.

Ellen

When the dream comes back
she's eight years old again and late, as
usual.
The morning is still dark,
the room frosty.
Ice crystals glitter on the windows.
The fire is out,
and Fern lies shivering
and vulnerable beneath her covers,
afraid to move.

The house is silent
(except for the tick-tock of the clock
growing louder—).
The house is silent
(except for the clock and her heart
thumping, thumping—
and the softest snores from Ellen
still sleeping—burrowed under the quilt).

In the dream,
Fern is once again alone,
and in charge of the morning.
And she's running late—rushing, but
unable
to move quickly enough
to make the meager lunches,
(raw-potato sandwiches
with bacon grease
on thick homemade bread).

She's late but unable
to get Ellen, her six-year-old sister,
to wake up,
to get her breakfast of cold oatmeal,
to get her dressed
in their warmest leggings,
threadbare socks,
and worn buttoned shoes,
to layer the sweaters knitted by Mama
under coats from the thrift
over wool skirts down to their knees
for the mile-long walk to school
up the icy road
in the dark.

Mama was out early
for her housecleaning job,
Daddy away protecting his sheep
from winter's bitter cold,
older sister, Fuchsia, now away.

Fern's panic now growing, she can't move
quickly.
Time is sluggish against her will.
She's filled with frantic doubt and fear and
heavy responsibility. Too much
for a child to mother a child.

So much to do. Too much to hold.

Life is bare and unforgiving.
Anxiety fills her dream
like a growing cloud of dark smoke
that she can't see her way through

until she wakes in a burst of sweat—
and with a jolt
she realizes she is grown, and safe.

Dear Family,

I was remembering when Ellen and I lived in this one old man's house when Mom cooked for him during the buckeroo and hay times. I even drove the old horse, helping hay one year. I rode the horse that went forward pulling a rope hooked to a big rake that grabbed a bite of hay. I'd drive and ride the old horse forward, pulling the fork with a big bite, center it on top of the haystack, wait till they got it all lined up and they got out of the way. Then they would signal me to back up the horse, which slacked up the rope, and they released the fork and dropped the hay. I'd work all day with a crew of men—they would chew tobacco to keep their lips from cracking, and mine just swelled up and got sore. It was hot and dry and sometimes dusty—but always fun and different.

Love you all so much,

Ma

Old Enough

As a young girl,
Fern loved school—
giggling with friends,
the rhythm of basketball
on the lacquered wood
of the old gym, the velvet gleam
of the borrowed saxophone
she played in the band.

She wasn't the best student—life was
too full and interesting
to focus
only on books.

But her family needed money,
so, when she was just fourteen,
they sent her away

to live
with an old woman ravaged by stroke
on a desolate farm
in the dry Oregon desert.

It was a job; she was old enough, and so
    she went

to nurse the old woman
forgotten by life—lingering
alone, somewhere
forgotten in Oregon.

Fern's heart fluttered with fear
when she first met her charge
hunched in a wheelchair,

the woman's frail body
bent and broken—
incontinent and incapable.

Silent and slumped in the cool shadows of
    a darkened room,

the woman's once-strong spirit
now angry and trapped,
bitter and shamed.

She had a lopsided face,
was unable to feed herself
and barely able to speak—
except to bark
her constant displeasure.

Her eyes lifted to meet Fern's fear
and, deep in the sorrow,
Fern saw the soul
within the woman's withered body.

Fern gathered her courage,
tenderly wiped the old lady's chin,
tucked the blanket around her
frail shoulders,
and brushed the strands of white hair
away from the fading and
watery blue eyes.

Together they moved out onto the porch;
out into the sunshine.

Onward.

The Calling

Fern found her purpose
in nursing school.
She loved learning with
her best friend, Dorothy.
They lived in Mother Merrill's house
just up the road from
St. Luke's Hospital.

Through late-night study sessions,
endless rounds with
cranky nuns, grateful patients,
brusque doctors, and kind mentors,
she discovered her gifts
and found her boundaries;
used her creativity
and compassion
in ways she'd never dreamed of.

Daily challenges, problems solved,
possibilities dreamed,
limitations overcome—

nursing was her calling,
her salvation, her lifelong pride.
The strict training forged skills
from her innate nature
and paved a lifelong path
of fulfillment.

She was a proud nurse
when she met and
began her life with Oscar.

Dear Fuchsia,

It's good to remember that you're not too many miles away, but we keep changing, and some changes bring tremors to our lives. Right now, I'm feeling so much better than I have for several years. I am more quiet within me, and it helps to direct my activities.

*The last tragedy in my life was I got a permanent! If no greater things shake me, I needn't worry! But, oh my gosh! I've known some doggies to crawl under the bed to hide when they get a new short grooming. I, too, wanted to crawl under a bed. Decades without a permanent set my very hair roots on end—rising up in objection! And the outcome was a haystack (NOT baled!) in a windstorm! In two days, I crawled out to face the public and got a short shingle—up the back, across the top, and down the temples. Anyway, it clings to my head, and it will grow out. But I feel like it changed my whole personality like as if I had layed [*sic*] my nose over to one side or a similar gross alteration.*

Love you, Sis.

Fern

Grit

Fern was the right partner for Oscar.
This feisty, creative, resilient,
sometimes infuriating woman
had the sturdy strength
and good humor
to bring order
out of chaos.

In the summer of 1950,
they packed their three children
and moved to
a remote gold-mining camp
in the boreal forest
of northern Canada.

North of Fort St. James—
up to the wilds of
Manson Creek, BC,
seeking gold.

Oscar in charge of the mine.
Fern as camp cook, and camp nurse—
mother to two young daughters,
five and two,
and a newborn son.

Living in a drafty cabin
without running water;
potty training in an outhouse
Don't drop me way down there, Ma,
driving the Jeep over swollen creeks

140 miles into "town" or
eight miles down a rutted road
to meet the mail plane
as it touched down
once a week at
Germansen Landing
on the Omineca River,
bringing news from home.

She cheerfully served and healed—
healed tough miners—
stitches numbed only by ice—
and served make-do menus
morning, noon, and evening
to her babies and men.

Wild animals and wilder beauty
surrounded her—
the threat of black bear and
roaming moose,
biting deerflies
that brought blood down
tender baby napes,
the constant battle with squirrels and
mice
in the storehouse.

Hardship balanced against the rosy blush
of morning and the sigh of murmuring
trees at dusk; against midnight calls of the
owl and the rushing dance of cold
mountain streams.

Fern had the grit to thrive

in the adventure of a lifetime,
constantly meeting the challenges
of an unforgiving
and wonderful wildness.

The Artist

Fern's firstborn

Fern saw a reflection of herself
within her oldest daughter.

So much was difficult—
the world just looks different
from the creative's
point of view.
Different and so often
misunderstood.
Guided by a fierce and free spirit
struggling to be seen.

So, her daughter
learned in her own way.
Time ran at its own pace—
her eye saw lines
and colors and texture
colliding and overlapping
a cacophony of wonder;
interesting new paths
to pursue.

Her hands shaped the world she saw
into surprising works of art
always a step beyond or
in front of or
behind the boundaries;
focus came and
went—flitting with the
intrusion of possibilities,

weaving emotions
and ideas
and distractions
into the art
of her life.

Fern saw her daughter.
And she supported her with love
in navigating the turmoil
of her gifts.

The Musician

Fern's middle daughter

Music ran through every vein
of her middle daughter.

From early Danish roots
music coursed generations
from great-great-grandfather
to great-grandmother—
then was shipped with the beloved
piano across the sea
to the Idaho ranch.

Always, the music flowed.
An uninterrupted line
of notes and measures
of beauty and song.

Passing on through
her grandmother
and then to her father—Oscar,
a classical pianist in his own right—
and carried to his daughter
for a lifetime of melody
within her soul.

Ancestral rhythms pulsing
through her heart—
longing to be sung
through the poetry
of her words.

The Sailor

Fern's son

Her son—now a man so much like his
father
at home upon the water.

Standing proud—braced against the wind,
hair rippled back;
anxious, protective eyes
scanning the horizon.

The sturdy hull of his creation
gently rolling with the waves,
ballasted by glowing layers of
carefully curated woods
sanded, shellacked, and buffed,
tightly fitted with gleaming brass—
catching the sun.

A cabinetmaker's art alive on the sea.

New sails snap and billow above—
clean white against a cloudless blue sky,
swelling with the breeze
carrying his hopes
and his little family
on the maiden voyage
as his dream
casts off.

The Mother

Fern's baby's babies

Her youngest daughter found her calling
as a mother to nine.
God provided his blessing
again and again and again.

Upstairs, in the old brass bed
Fern's newborn granddaughter
greets the world, red-faced and
full-throated—startled by the light,
the final desperate push,
and sudden pain
as her tiny lungs
fill with air—

she enters an unfamiliar world—
new senses assaulted
with a cacophony of sound,
pungent with the smell of blood,
tasting the juices of the womb
as her lips seek
comfort from the
breast.

Fern gently wraps
her granddaughter
and stills her cries.
A circle once again completed
in the old brass bed
that sits nestled in the eaves
between the sturdy logs
of her safe home.

Oscar

Fern's partner

Oscar was a mining engineer,
a student of geology
devoted to the hills;
a collector of rare rocks and gold coins.
He was a proud naval officer,
a lifelong seeker of adventure;
a classical pianist, a goofy performer,
the lead in college plays,
a bit actor in the movie *The Northwest*
Passage;
a hole-in-one golfer, skier, swimmer,
and a recognized leader in his field.

Oscar possessed a quick wit and stoic
strength.
He was an engineer but so much more.
And he loved Fern.

Fern, his wife, was his can-do partner
for thirty-three years.
She shared his love of nature,
his artistic sense, his adventurous spirit.
And she followed where he led.

She was camp nurse and cook,
gardener, singer of silly cowboy songs,
corporate wife,
busy mother to their four children,
eventual "Gaga" to sixteen grandchildren,
everyone's friend.

And then, too young, Oscar died,
too young to reap the harvest
of their complicated life together,
leaving her alone
to begin again
to find her own path,
and follow where it led.

Quest

After Oscar died
Fern took the *QE2* across the rolling seas,
boarding in New York to sail
into the waiting arms
of her daughter's family
on the shores of France,
then on to Germany.

On deck she felt the salt
spray against her face,
and bravely greeted each dawn,
gazing for days
at a watery horizon.

Rolling waves against the bow rocking,
    gently rocking.
Imagining. Dreaming.

Then, on solid ground in a new land,
she found a cornucopia of wonders—
new language, music, history,
fields of pasture,
steep mountains,
and fortified castles.

Artisans of the glass offered shards of
    beauty—
the finest stained glass
to reward her quest to find the right
    green,
translucent blue, vibrant red,

glowing yellow—
a treasure hunt for a sunset
or a meadow
to carry home;
and assemble
a beginning to rebuild her life
piece by piece.

Fern's Pond

1976–1989

When she found the pond and saw her profile against the cliff overlooking the valley, Fern's heart overflowed with wonder. It was clear to her that she was home. That place was her dream come true, and she was determined to manifest her vision.

On Fern's Pond, she felt safe, inspired, and renewed. Crystal-clear springs bubbled from under the rocks at a constant forty-five to fifty degrees—feeding the quiet waters that offered sanctuary in the harsh desert. The lush edges of the pond sheltered tender sprouts of new grass, the emerging blades of cattails, mosses, algae, and an abundance of worms, grubs, insects, frogs, and tiny snails sufficient to nourish a growing flock of mallards—as well as rainbow trout, muskrats, and snakes. And it was perfect for growing the reeds and willows and grasses she needed for basketmaking.

Yet the dry, sagebrushed grounds around it begged for attention. Something stirred within her—a longing to embrace the forlorn land; to wrap her arms around it, gather it in, nurture it, and bring life into its dry and neglected soil. Maybe it was a connection to her childhood, or maybe it was the nurse in her with an instinct to care and soothe and heal. Whatever it was, she sensed both a familiarity and a wild calling of new possibilities as she breathed in the clear air and surveyed the landscape.

Fern began to ingest life with great gulps—bonding her spirit to the land—and together they began to blossom. Her imagination flourished as she expressed her creative instincts. It was as if she had finally been given access to life's banquet, and she was determined to devour all that she had secretly longed for as far back as she could recall.

All her ancestral voices rose up in unity with her—willing dormant seeds to sprout, coaxing the sleeping earth to wake, and then gently bedding it down to sleep through winter. And the wild and domestic creatures she nurtured brought vibrant energy to the unfolding seasons.

She learned her way into her dream—trusting in her pioneering instincts, determined to use her problem-solving skills to improvise, undeterred by mistakes, not afraid to ask for help and try again—always propelled by endless enthusiasm and indomitable optimism. Even with limited resources, she always managed to get by—even thrive.

And she reveled in every visit from her children and grandchildren as her "home" for them took shape. The only legacy that mattered was that her grandchildren would one day come to know her place as "home." Her silent prayer was to live long enough and strong enough to cement that bond for generations.

Summer and Fall

The Basket Maker

Fern stands still, sturdy, and resolute,
surveying the day's offerings.

White hair tucked beneath a
khaki knit cap from some forgotten war,
red flannel shirt over denim jeans—
her black high-top tennis shoes
give good protection against
the nettles that line the path—
gloves and clippers in hand.

She's a weaver of baskets,
and it's time to imagine.
She sets out to find "something
    interesting. . . ."

Today's search yields:
one dried seedpod from a silkweed plant,
five horsetails with tough striped stems,
three iridescent blue and green feathers
from the old mallard,
and a handful of twining grapevines—
saved from the burn pile.

Reaping complete, she commences.

She soaks the dry grasses
and stripped willow bark until they're
    pliant,
then lays out the foundation and threads,

testing the strands for resilience,
tossing the frayed, saving the strong.

She works as she lives—
sensing for patterns,
taking the rough with the smooth,
the dried with the fresh,
the tangled with the simple,
the scarred with the unblemished.

She's dazzled but undaunted
by the complexity of possibilities.
She seeks an essence, a through line
to bring coherence to the jumble
of what she's gathered.

Her fingers are her tools—
gnarled and nimble,
gentle yet strong.

She lays one strand against the other,
taking up the warp and weft
against a sturdy core.

In and out; over and beneath—
she transforms nature into art,
selecting accents for character, texture,
and a touch of color;
blending the subtle and the bold
into an object
of humble elegance.

She weaves with intention and intuition
until, at last, a basket
emerges, tight and sturdy
with a simple beauty.

Open yet complete.

Dear Family,

I finished up four large willow baskets I was making for an order. The gal is an artist from Twin and has made large white geese with little hats on them and wanted me to make the "nests." The nests were about fifteen to eighteen inches across and three to four inches deep. My fingers got so sore! I made them in three days. Besides, while gathering willows, I poked my right eye and it got all bloody and I have looked weird for two weeks this coming Wednesday. Still hasn't absorbed—but it doesn't hurt a bit.

I am making some beautiful baskets. I want to have about fifty to take to Jackpot next May. Carl is having the Artisans of the Snake—of which I am a member now—put on a show down there. Everyone will have paintings but me—he thinks my baskets will go well. Seems like I've sure got them fooled around here—so, of course, I work like mad so they won't find me out!

Ma

Tiger Swallowtail

Flickering sunshine and
shadow, the swallowtail
dances with shy daisies and
wild red paintbrush,
fluttering—flirting
with the tempting clover
that grows
between garden rows—
tender and plump with
nectar and morning dew.

Flashing butterfly wings—a tiger's stripes
on powdered silk;
a dash of summer joy
rippling through the green.
A gift of gold
waving to the sky,
lighting up the shade
and spreading
sweet comfort.

Flying butter.

Ants (1)

The ants go marching,
source to home, source to home,
source to home to source again.

The anthill grows,
grain upon grain
above an underground labyrinth
of chambers and tunnels,
passages and highways,
a universe unseen
by the passing
lizard or snake.

They excavate. Construct. Repair.

With endless toil,
singular focus, and
supernatural strength,
they haul twigs and leaves
for the nest, soil and sand
for the hill, scavenging detritus
from the land,
building and rebuilding.

The days march on
through eons of evolution.
But the ants remain
steadfast in their purpose, committed
to the directive

passed from generation to generation,
as old as the dinosaurs,
one grain at a time.

Kites

As she turned onto the gravel road
leading to the house, her heart
beat faster. She knew
her two towheaded grandsons
waited there.

And as she turned the corner,
a leap of her heart!
There they were in the yard,
flying the bright kites
she had bought them.

Something so simple yet so profound:
They were flying the kites she'd bought
them.

She had pictured it so,
as she stood in the drugstore aisle,
wondering if this kite or that.
Deciding, at last, on both.
One for each.

She would join her grandsons,
and they would have a moment.
She would join them,
and they would have an afternoon—
they would share a memory.

She stood and watched.
Her heart soared with the kites

as the tails caught the breeze—
out over the sheep wagon,

beyond the edge of the lawn,
above the cherry trees and the old locusts,
pausing to hover over
the vineyard and garden
that sloped down toward the pond.

The kites continued their lift—
successfully launched,
sent aloft, perhaps, by her silent prayer
for a good and gentle wind.

Then, a sudden shift—a gust
caught the kite held by the younger one
and twisted and tugged at the line,
wrenching it free.

An anguished cry.
A wail ascended on the wind—
Runaway kite!

Without hesitation—in visceral reaction
Fern, herself, launched.
Across the garden,
down to the vineyard,
through the dry nettles she raced.

Nylon stockings snagging, jacket flung
    aside,
skirt hiked up, town shoes discarded,
she flew in blind pursuit
of the errant kite.

Despair rose upon the wind
as a draft from the edge of the pond
caught the kite and
bobbed it toward the open field beyond—
it would be irretrievable.

But, miraculously,
the old willow guarding the edge
of the lower pond
reached up and caught it—
kept it tangled and safe

while Fern
scaled the rough branches,
barefoot and torn,
whooping and grateful—
and delivered it safely back home.

Mud Cakes

She sits alone in the shade of the gazebo
smiling at the solitary scene
untouched since last Sunday
now filled with memories
of children's laughter.

She sees them splashing
in the slumped wading pool
that lies partially deflated
and forgotten
at the edge of the grass.

In her thoughts,
she watches them stagger,
back and forth from
the pool to the toolshed,
sloshing their cargo of water
from the red plastic bucket

into the powdery dust
as they carry out their work—
making dough from dirt
in the chipped enamel bowl
they unearthed in the old chicken coop.

She hears them, their busy make-believe,
their earnest pursuit of
baking mud cakes
and brewing grass tea.
Preparing her feast.

Measuring just the right amount
of wet soil and dandelion fluff,
a pinch of this, a tad of that—
patting perfect little cakes into shape
with their perfect little hands.

With care, they arrange their offering
on a weathered cedar plank
decorated with willow leaves,
three special rocks,
and daisies,

then deliver it to her with shy efficiency
    and solemn care.

She tastes each one thoughtfully,
smacking her lips in appreciation.
Compliments to the chef!
A tip for the excellent service!
Would she like more . . . ?
Please. Yes . . . please.
More. Much more.

They had toiled until the sun
began to sear the cloudless sky—
singeing their cheeks
and forcing their reluctant retreat
into afternoon naps.

Then to begin their long journey back
    home away from her
again—

leaving behind muddy footprints,
an overturned bowl,
a lopsided pool,
and wilted daisies baking in the heat
of the last summer days.

Dear Family,

Time to catch up!

I'm making bread rolls tonight for a Saturday dinner at the lodge and will furnish fifteen pounds of potatoes from my garden. It's a dinner we are putting on for a reunion of some kind for someone I don't know! Anyway, my rolls are rolling up over the edge of the bowl and it's midnight—time out—will have to finish this later.

OK—it's later. Got fifty rolls in one pan and another small pan for samples. This morning early, I got up and picked string beans. Then went to town to get more fliers [sic] *printed for the art festival coming up. Returned home and napped two hours. Then I made twenty-one pints of apricot-pineapple jam and six pints of pickled beets. Took a chunk of chocolate cake to my neighbor and brought back a big bowl of raspberries. Washed dishes twice in my sink, and it's still full.*

I'm going to butcher my geese this fall. They go through my flower garden playing that game "I won't bite you; I won't bite you..." as they proceed to smash them with their big feet, and then they say, "But I WILL bite YOU!" and off comes the head of the dearest flowers. I got seven new rosebushes this spring, and they eat the blossoms as soon as they come on. The ducks don't do that. My veggie garden is fenced, or I wouldn't have any.

Anyway, I want you to know I'm pretty stable on my living. My chickens are multiple, and I sell some eggs. I butchered four lambs, sold one to Billy, and made enough to cover the expense of butchering and wrapping for all of them. So my locker is full—stuffed! I have hooked up the old trailer just like old days and coaxed my two beautiful Suffolk ewes in to go get bred. They are now off in a pasture with a bunch of lambs and a huge beautiful purebred Suffolk buck. (Good luck, buck!) While they are gone, I must cement rocks up around the corner of their *pen because it keeps giving away [*sic*]. Then I will build a little lambing shelter for spring.*

Much love,

Ma

Hi, all of you!

A lovely new fence is now built around my large locust grove, and I will soon get my two ewe sheep in there for the winter. It'll make a nice duck place also. The fence comes all the way up from the main road around the trees and slants down to the water where the trees end. My two ewe sheep will lamb in the spring. I'll build them a shelter with straw (like the pigs' house that the wolf huffed and puffed on). I hope my fence will keep the coyotes out. An electric wire was installed underground from my place up to the spud cellar so I have light in there. Also, they put a light in my chick house and the grain part of it too.

I took a tole painting class, canned a lot, killed four roosters and froze them, etc. I got a small spinning wheel—new one—and I have learned to clean and card and spin the lambs' wool. I finished the macramé hanging and I hung it by the fireplace from the upstairs beam. Now, I'm making a macramé lampshade for over the table.

My neighbor caught fifteen fish, and we caught two rock chucks in the trap! Last week, I saw a rock chuck scamper from my garden. In two days, it ate four head of cauliflower! I couldn't believe it—first cauliflower I've ever grown—gone! It didn't bother my tomatoes and cabbage but ate my carrots down to an inch high—three times! Old-timers say they are about to hibernate now, so I will plant a late garden of turnips, rutabagas, parsnips, lettuce, etc.

Much love,

Ma

Abundance

She was hungry with her whole being,
so she grew her own feast.

Squash and cucumbers and tomatoes,
yellow and orange and green and red,
twining together on their mounds.
Russet potatoes deep in the dark moist
earth,
crisp lacy lettuce, rich kale, and tender
spinach,
carrots and beets for pulling and pickling,
apples and apricots and cherries for pies,
plump raspberries and strawberries as big
as your palm.

—

Picnic for one on a clear August day
in the shade of the gazebo
she built herself.

She sets the tin pitcher overflowing with
yellow sunflowers
on the worn blue Danish tablecloth,
and pours chilled white wine (from her
vineyard)
into an antique cut-crystal glass.
On the painted Japanese platter
she lays sliced tomatoes

(still warm from the sun),
crisp cucumber-and-radish sandwiches
(on thick slices of homemade bread),
juicy, golden apricots,
and cheese from her goat—
(a fat wedge, hand-pressed).

Picnic for one—on this clear August
    day—
served on her new red apple plates.

Apple Pies

She gathers apples
in the orchard
from the gnarled and twisted tree.

The heavy branches dipped low—
offering their fruitful gifts
to the ants and birds and worms.

She gathers apples
in the fresh morning,
carefully cupping them in a dish towel,

tied around her waist
until it is sagging
from the weight.

And then: a bit of magic.
Cinnamon, sugar, a pinch of salt,
lard to make a tender crust.

Finally, sixteen bubbling pies
sit cooling on the sills
ready for the neighbors.

Dear Ones,

I have a gorgeous vineyard, and 160 grapevines cause quite a lot of attention. The posts are good wood posts and line up from the different angles just like a vineyard should. Since I put them in, I have placed three different orders for grapes (100 vines in one order!). My grapes are doing so well—some twining the top wire (4 ft). Grapes are forming—a few here and there. Mostly they are clean and look beautiful and are bug free because the chickens eat bugs all day long.

I went out to get the last of my garden produce in and found a whole half bushel of gourds hanging in the weeds—never dreamed there were so many! I have canned twenty-eight half gallons of tomatoes. Have a lot of carrots to can and applesauce to make. I made twelve quarts of mincemeat—best stuff ever! A woman gave me a surplus of cabbage that was about to freeze in the garden. Only thirty heads—so I made seventy-two quarts of sauerkraut.

I got a huge pumpkin for Halloween from my favorite gardener. I could hardly put my arms around it! I cut it up and made pumpkin pie mix, cooked and canned it—got eight quarts and made eight pies besides. The seeds were so big, I soaked them and roasted them, and they taste better than the sunflower seeds and aren't as small to eat either.

I'm keeping busy!

Ma

Night Walking

Her night sweats rise again,
drowning the boundaries
between restless sleep and fevered
    waking.

So, she goes out among the moonlit rows

where late-August grapes
hang heavy on the vine,
their swollen fruits
and tendrils hiding
deep among the shadows.

She glides across the hushed and sleeping
    land,

her nightgown
stained by tender tears that freshly
fall and glisten
on the swollen hanging orbs
and leathered leaves.

Her trailing hem snags upon the hidden
    vines;

its silken threads pull—then stall—
the churning thoughts
and old laments.
She breathes . . . as moonlight soothes her
troubled heart.

She wanders barefoot down narrow
    vineyard rows

and the damp night soil,
cool between her toes,
caresses and comforts her soul
as she walks swaddled
by the gentle light.

And crickets sing their ceaseless song.

She Dances Alone

She dances alone in the dark
to the music from her dreams,
no lover to hold in her arms.
The dawn is still hidden
in the stars
as she hugs her heart
against her chest.

She dances alone in the dawn,
bathed in the light of the past,
heart aching for youth,
body pining with passion
for human touch.
Gently swaying
in her wrinkled skin.

In the afternoon, she dances alone
on that one narrow sunbeam
that streams across her floor,
a golden banister
she could slide down, glide down
into the puddle
where the light has pooled.

She dances alone in the growing dusk
by the glow of her fireplace
as it flickers against the wall.
Dancing, swaying with contentment,
grateful for the jazz—
the improvisation
of life unfolding.

My dear family,

I don't know whether to tell you guys this—but you'd feel bad if I kept things from you. I'm going back to nursing at the hospital in Gooding. I start Monday—at six dollars an hour. It is a small, very clean, well-equipped hospital, and as long as my health is good, I may as well make some money. I am so glad to be working for now, so don't worry. The money comes in handy—but, beyond that, there is a tremendous satisfaction in working. I don't need help financially. There is no sense using gas running to town to eat too much with the old ladies and waste time I could be using more productively. Besides, I've been missing the hospital talk and the bustle. So, my nursing will be good all around!

Nursing deepened her sense of purpose, and as the months unfolded, brought a new rhythm and satisfaction to her days.

My basketmaking has come to a halt lately because of work, but I must get busy again. I had a bit of adjustment to make at first—just wanted to come home and rest after work. But there was always some function to go to. Now it's all shaping up, and I get enough rest. I get home about 3:30 and nap for an hour or two, then get up and buzz for a while. Days are getting warmer and longer. I go to work in the a.m. just as dawn is sneaking up in the east. I haven't had any bad roads. I get up at 5 a.m., have a leisurely hour of coffee and quiet, and take off at 6 a.m., go a slow pace and get to Gooding at 6:30. I get the night report at 6:45 and then the eight-hour shift is on.

I like working at the hospital. I'm in charge when I'm on—start intravenous lines, have the pharmacy keys, and dispense drugs when necessary. It takes me into a different world two days a week. I am now making seven dollars and seventy cents an hour. But it's awfully nice on the days I don't have to go. I told the supervisor that she could schedule me to work if I could get relief if I was needed at home. She said she'd work for me anytime I had to leave—so I'm OK there. Things are not so bad, really. I had just gotten myself so darn spoiled—running around spending money! Things are different now. It's not hurting me.

Love, Ma

Dear Ones,

Now I am working on the stained glass windows for my library doors. I am using all the beautiful glass pieces that we bought in Germany, and I am quite excited about the design. I am quite encouraged about the progress, though, and as I keep working, I gain confidence, and it's getting easier.

My new doors are a great joy to me for I have time to feel my way with them. I have the project on my kitchen table—often work on it before I have my morning coffee, and many people come to survey it and watch it grow. Many techniques and supplies and working tools have changed since I first tried to make a window—I have profited by going slow and learning.

It is a very big undertaking and beyond my acquired training, but I'm learning and enjoying the challenge. I become better at cutting, fitting, filing, every day. My colors are coming together peacefully. All the glass pieces have to be cut, then fitted closely together. When all are cut, they each have to be wrapped with a quarter-inch foil. Then a liquid or paste wiped over the foil, then soldered together. There are over one hundred pieces. I will get only the one window done this year. It is on a big plyboard, so it can be transported to under the bed if not finished when company comes next summer.

Lots of love,
Ma

Library Doors

Fern selects each translucent piece and
solders it into place—
carefully creating a still life
curated from shards.
The seasons unfold—across the double
 stained glass doors
that open to her library.

On the left,
reds and oranges and yellows
blaze against the pale gray sky
where sienna branches lace the
 foreground.
Winter tones mute the palette
and light the shadows
with the silence of cream and gray.

On the right,
spring unfurls in a cacophony of greens
 and lilac,
and summer basks under a golden sun.
Plump grapes hang heavy on the vineyard
 rails
and cirrus streaks against the aqua sky
reflect in the depths
of a glassy pond.

And the trailing marble walk leads your
 eye
along a winding path . . .
beyond, beyond. . . .

Winter and Spring

New Snow

Snow fell
silently for hours, uninterrupted,
obscuring the moon
that now hangs low above the horizon.
Snow whispered all night long
murmuring through the trees,
covering the path.

Flake by flake it filled
each naked branch of the lacy maple
embracing the old house.
Crystals balanced on every slender twig
and cupped the top of
the single quivering seedpod
still hoping for spring.

Now, bright morning sun
glints outside her window.
Glassy chandeliers
catch early beams.
The clean unblemished path
waits for new footprints
down to the pond.

My dear family,

How comforting to have a stack of hay, a bag of grain, and a pile of fireplace wood. This zero weather isn't a worry. Without a lot of snow piled up, I can go and come. I keep the car heater plugged in, and she takes off easy. I was low for a couple weeks—just had that intestinal trouble, and it made me weak and no good for pep. I got through all the chores in due time and good shape, though I wanted to stay in bed sometimes. I have just been hanging in close to home, keeping our pipes from freezing.

The trappers have quit coming. They did catch a small raccoon and brought it to me dead. So I'm starting to skin it out. It is frozen again now. Besides that, it is porcupine time, and Callows have brought me five porcupines frozen. Soon as I can, I'll pluck out the best quills. I have wide-nose pliers for the job.

I wish I could just lock up the house and come see you. But this is my home, and I do love it. I've taken time this winter to just look out the windows and enjoy the ducks, watch the sunset, and listen to the owls at night when the moon is light and no wind blowing. Or sit and eat breakfast in my warm sunroom at the break of dawn. I keep it warm because I work in there a lot late at night. I keep the heat turned low in the center of the house and warm it mostly by the fireplace during the day. I must write more often because when I share these things, I don't feel like I'm living alone.

Love always,

Ma

Collections

From scarcity came a compulsion to
 collect—

assembling a collage of a life
in all its longed-for fullness
creating an archive of stories
that were never told—
stories continually patched and repatched,
filling the holes—
shoring up the silence
or drowning out the voices
of her past.

Affirmations that she could, at last,
reach out and attain what had been
beyond her childhood grasp.

Collections as varied as her unbound
 curiosity.

Antiques—bubbled bottles, carved
 furniture,
a set of leaded-glass dishes.
Tatted lace doilies and hand-stitched
broad tablecloths from the old country.
Rusted tiny metal trucks and
wooden slingshots
once treasured by small hands.

One—no two—actually three wood-
 burning stoves

burnished and shined;
now draped to preserve their iron beauty.

Dolls by the dozens carefully tucked in an
 old trunk—
delicate porcelain dolls, rag dolls, wood
 dolls,
dolls dressed in costume from other
 lands.
One doll from 1895 with two left feet.
Boxes and frames of arrowheads,
some as big as your fist;
others tiny as a fingernail.
Pieces of stained glass—
translucent or bubbled, rippled or flat
colored by the mysteries of
European mineral alchemy
ready to be assembled.

Tubes of oil paints from a forgotten artist;
bags of charcoal bits from the same.
An easel, just in case, you never know.
Artist's notebooks filled with rough
 sketches
of profiles and delicate drawings
of the arches of a finger
refined over and over and over
until just right.

Taxidermied animals—
two buffalo heads, a mongoose and cobra,
various birds, an antelope head;
un-taxidermied small birds

waiting to be stuffed by her skillful
    hands—
stiff and waiting
in the pump room freezer.

And also Oscar's collections:
gold and silver dollars;
Early American pennies and limited-
    edition sets;
pesos, yen, krone, freshly minted
    Deutsche marks,
each tucked in their own transparent
    sleeve.
Stamps from every country visited
by children, friends, or relatives.
A case of rare rocks, minerals, and fossils.

Oscar's WWII medals and uniforms.
Intricate wood carvings from China,
lengths of silk for kimonos,
taut stretches of silk from Japan—
lightly feathered with calligraphy,
    bamboo,
and cherry blossoms reaching
across trifold screens.

Baby clothes—tiny receiving gowns and
    booties
carefully laundered and saved for forty
    years
in packages labeled for each of her
    children.
Her son's Vietnam ribbons,
khakis, and ID dog tags.

Pressed leaves and native flowers
from her 4-H leader days
now grayed and crumbling
between the yellowing pages of aging
    newsprint.
Crayon drawings and macaroni pictures
    and
first hand-scribbled love notes
from grandchildren.

Every paper clipping, graduation
    program, yearbook,
and photo taken
carefully scrapbooked and stored
for a walk down memory lane
at some future time
in some imagined moment
with someone who never came.

My dear family,

What a long time since I have written! So much has gone past—lately I've been getting up early in order to catch up on things. It is now 5:30, and I've washed a pan of porcupine quills, cleaned the bathroom, and made coffee. And now I'm propped up in bed, your pictures are looking at me, and I'm on my way to writing to you.

The porcupine quills I just got plucked were from a real old animal—some quills are four inches long! The porcupines were trapped at Carl's place. An old feller friend of mine came and asked if I wanted them. I went with him up the Malad Canyon back of the rock house of Hayden's—snow above our knees—and together we got the three animals, stuffed them in gunnysacks, and dragged and carried them off the hill. They have been frozen a week, but lately the thaw has come and I've had to take care of them.

I've been asked to get together a private showing of my baskets and jewelry and show this spring. I'm making some good-looking baskets now. Going to use some beads and quills to decorate.

Mom

Snapshots

(On a winter evening by the light of the
fireplace, memories splayed around
her on the floor. . . .)

Sisters, forever young
in black and shades of gray
hopeful and clear-eyed.

Oscar, his wild hair in waves,
cocky on the running board
of their '38 Ford.

Proud new nurse in a starched white cap
with her best friend, Dorothy,
on their graduation day.

Bucking hay on the Idaho ranch,
wrestling calves to brand
in the summer sun.

Silhouetted against the sails,
headed to Alaska,
her son proudly at the helm.

Kimonos under cherry clouds
blooming in Kyoto.
Toddler grandsons hugging close.

Summer cats and downy chicks
hiding in blanket tents,
a campground in the house.

Baby girl born in the old brass bed—
a miracle of life
from her own baby girl.

Paper Angels

Carefully, Fern unwraps each wrinkled
paper angel.
She smooths the glittered, curling wings
and straightens the lopsided halos
that frame the crayon smiles
and penciled winking eyes.

Next, the clothespin soldiers
dressed smartly in red jackets
and sharp black pants
markered on with a toddler's precision.
A proud black pom-pom hat
holds each head high.
Ready to serve.

In the background, a tape recording
reels Christmas carols
sung by her faraway little family.
The children's voices
blend with unsteady lyrics—
a symphony of enthusiastic
disharmony.

Fern smiles—alone—through her tears;
gently places each silent singing angel
and each smart saluting soldier
on its own naked bough.

At last, lifting the tattered papier-mâché
star

with tinseled tips and fraying fringe—
she crowns the top.

And the hopeful carols ring out, “Joy to
 the World.”

Lambing in Winter

The ground has hardened, crusted over
from a harsh winter
of freezing and thawing
slush and ice.
Freezing, thawing, freezing—waiting
suspended in the fallow days.
A slight scent of fireplace smoke floats
upon the night.
Spring is a distant dream.

Anticipation hangs heavy as
her thoughts fill with a distant memory
of her father's shepherd song,
the crack of his sagebrush fire,
and the bleating, bleating of his flock
as he watched over.

Darkness has silenced everything
except the distant swish of cars
on the highway above,
the neighbor's barking dog,
the crack of her boots
on the icy path to the shed,
and the bleating, bleating of the ewe,
close with lamb.

Alone in the dark,
Fern softly sings the old shepherd's song,
holding, watching, waiting, expectant
as the ewe's plaintive distress cuts the night.
Then, a fragile cry—

Dear Family,

On Thursday, my second ewe started to have her lamb at 7 a.m. My new neighbor came to tell me, knocking at my door, and I rushed out because I saw from my window that the old girl had just dropped her lamb, and it was a cold, frosty morn. I put on my big heavy coat and hood over my nightdress and went to cuddle the little one. It was small and shaking. The mother ate the sack away from it and stomped away. I gathered it up. Old mother never came back to claim it. So, I kept it warm while she pranced around wild-like, her afterbirth not yet delivered. The other three-week-old buck lambs would come to paw the little one or bunt it when I put it down. After hours of hoping it would survive and staying away, hoping the mother would claim it, I finally brought it into the warm bathroom and eventually fed it some warm, diluted, canned milk. I would often return it to the mother's quarters and place it so she could claim it—but, no sir! She would have nothing to do with it but bunt it and knock it down. It rolled down the hill, and the two bucks pranced up, bunting it and pawing at it. I kept it in the house overnight.

By that time, I was accepted as its mother, and Rowdy let it sleep by him. On Friday, Wanda's sheep man came to "make the ewe accept the lamb." His idea was to put them in close quarters together. So I dug out the granary, piled some things (a tent, a box of wool, and a can of kerosene on the shelf) to clear the floor. We pulled and pushed and shoved the old ewe into the shed and I carried the baby and we left them alone together. A ruckus arose, and the door bulged. I peeped in the window and saw the wool over the floor, the tent there, too, and the kerosene spilling all over the place. I opened the door, beat the old ewe's snout to keep her back, and pawed all that kerosene-soaked wool out into the chicken pen.

When I unearthed the lamb, it was hardly breathing. I brought it in the house and nursed it all night, but it went ahead and died. I called Wanda's man and said, "Come get this ewe off my place—you can have her!"

Anyway, Saturday morning, at the crack of dawn, the other ewe started having trouble with her labor. I never saw one struggle so! She'd lay [sic] *on her side and with each seizure all four legs would fly off the ground. So, off I go to help her! On my arrival, I saw a tiny foot and nose dangling out of the ewe. She made it to her feet—frantic and I was too! So, I came in and called Tim—but before he arrived, the rest of the lamb was expelled, and the mother was eating the sack.*

She loved the lamb from the start. Being a new mother, she didn't know how the baby needed to nurse. Never before had I had any trouble with lambs this way. I was finally able to catch and throw her down and unplug her nipples, and the lamb sucked some colostrum. She still ran from the baby, so I brought it in and fed it, then put it back out with its mother.

She did love that little one—murmuring to it and licking it. And old sheepy stood still and baby filled her hungry stomach!

Ma

Beauty in the Blight

Do not look for perfection.
There is beauty in the blight—
badges of resilience;
stories told in scars.

Ruffled leaves curl around
the insects
whose hunger laced
through tender growth—
tatted lace that now admits the dappled
light dancing
in the shadows.

Crusty lichens and soft moss
take their hold
where death has descended,
clinging to the ridged trunks,
filling in the rough.

Winter's naked limbs
unadorned against the sky
weave their exposed fingers
into a filigree of black—

Scalloped sears on emerging edges
hold the brand of winter's late frost,
when buds dared trust too soon—
their tender cores exposed.

And still spring blossoms start anew to
push their hopeful petals
into the warming sun.

Simple Joy

That moment. That exquisite, sacred
moment.

As tender buds push past
the last of winter's crust
cleaving from the dormant past
leaving behind the confines
of a discarded shell;
no longer encased—

seeking the warmth
of a spring day
reaching for the promise
of possibilities
wrapped in a drop of
rainbow morning dew
and emerge

resilient and hopeful,
welcoming the freedom,
the transition
to a new day,
a new life
bathed
in light.

That moment. That exquisite, sacred
moment.
Rebirth.

Family,

I'm beginning to get caught up on things around here. Outside work is going slow, but I have a lot of garden in—new grass coming up—corn a couple inches up. I've got a milker on the cow (electric!) and installed it myself. I let the calf in to nurse. She takes one whole quarter. Then I put her out and then hook up the milker to the cow, and I sit in the straw and watch! Soon as the milk quits pumping through the tubes, I pull the things off, put Bag Balm on, and turn her loose again. I put her out to pasture all day and keep her in at night. The calf stays in the pen during the day and in the stall at night when the cow is in the corral all night. I have regular customers that come here for the milk. When I get a little ahead on milk, I make cottage cheese and sell that. The milk goes right from the cow to container, so it is clean—not a bit of flake off the cow. It tastes so good—not a bit "cowy." I keep clean straw in the corral and ear tags to keep the flies away.

I'm figuring this out!

Ma

Dear Family,

Wildlife is wild around here! Soon as I get home, I turn the chickens out, gather the eggs, and feed the noisy ducks and geese. The ducks and geese come in squawking, as usual. Of the five babies, one turned up a drake—so now I have two drakes and six hen ducks! The geese stay with them always. I turned the chuckers loose, and they stay around the house to eat also. You should hear the happy chucking of my chicks when I turn them out to get bugs now. In the newly exposed ground, they dust and roll and sing.

Old papa goose chased his two white offspring away from the crowd, so they wander together alone. One is a male and one a female. They make a nice matched pair—like swans on the pond. Old papa has three gray geese females following him—I can tell the difference because they have a fluffier undertuft between their legs. I understand from "Old-Timers" that one can pluck that fluff off in the spring and it doesn't hurt them—just makes them mad. That's where down comforters originated from without killing the geese.

Also, my sheep are having twins—one more sheep to go! My band is seven now. One ewe hasn't produced yet. Also, I planted two junipers on the hillside and about one hundred irises all along the driveway.

Oh say, I must tell you—I got the Grange Citizen of the Year award! I will send the clipping. I was very proud and surprised. I'm not sure I deserve it, but I'll accept it gladly. Sure makes me feel good.

Love,

Ma

Stumps

Curious how
the raw stumps
of the old locust trees—
renewed by shy spring sunshine
are sprouting fresh green twigs
again.

Last fall,
the men she hired to "clean up the place"
had gotten carried away
and lopped the old gnarled trees
down to mere stumps.

Not just the upper branches,
broken from summer storms
and hanging dead and dangerous,
but all the good ones too—
gone.

The grove of proud locusts
guarding the corner of her drive
was sliced down to mere stumps.

So much so that, when she rounded the
corner
to drive up the lane,
her heart had lurched with pain
at the open sky that newly crowned
the fenced-in sheep pen.

The rude and artless denudement
insulted her senses—
wounding her heart.
And, with tears,
she began to apologize
for the assault . . .
to the pond and the pasture
and the blinking creatures hiding
between the open dry blades.

But, from the patience of winter
and the resilience of life,
spring grasses now fill in
the muddied ground,
the old ewe lazes in patches of sun, and
ducks find new refuge along the banks.

The open wounds of the raw stumps have
healed
and are sprouting strong green twigs
again.

Hey, kids,

I never told you that I got poison oak so bad on my legs. The ankles were a solid, weeping, scabby, itchy blob. Itch! Oh my gosh! I finally decided it wasn't from eating too many tomatoes. Gave in and went to the doc. He says, "What have you been doing for it?" I says, "You want me to go through the whole routine? I first put on aloe vera gel—started trimming the whole aloe vera plant and rubbing on the gel—used the neighbors' Caladryl up, then went to cornstarch, soda baths, Clorox baths." He stopped me there, says, "Hey, I can't take any more—stop!" I said, "Oh, Doctor, I haven't even gotten to the Fels-Naptha soap yet." Well, by that time I was so itchy also I couldn't sit on his table any longer, so he gave me a shot in the rear and a couple prescriptions and some tranquilizer. The bath stuff smelled and looked like old sheep dip—but one dipping for twenty minutes and all itching stopped. I went to sleep that night without even a tranquilizer.

But it didn't all clear up for another week. I sheep dipped three times a day and spread on the most delightfully soothing cream. As the swelling went down, it looked like elephant hide, and I am still dry and scaly. I'm glad I went to the doctor because Nora Barlogi said she knew a woman—got it up inside her and she had to be hospitalized—I didn't tell her it was already up my thighs and across my "whoopty" and I'd been doing some frantic digging when I was around the corner so no one could see me. So much for "on the farm" life! Ain't it excitin'?

Much love,

Ma

Gratitude

She sits in solitude on the back porch
in the warmth of the morning sun
of a new spring day
nursing her coffee.

She takes in all of it—
feeling the aliveness
of the land and the possibilities
for her dreams.

Absorbing the moment with grateful
    gulps. Content.

She sees the sprouting greens emerging
from last fall's plantings
and watches the eagles soar
in the clear air above the cliffs.

A cool breeze ruffles the edge of the pond,
teasing it to play.

Her sturdy raft lies anchored and
waiting at the edge of the pond;
striped trout lurk fat and lazy beneath
the mossy depths;

loyal ducks harvest snails,
and the steadfast spring robins
pull worms from the rich
and thawing soil
along the banks.

Fern takes it all in with wonder—
grateful for the living embrace
of all she has nurtured—

bravely weaving the
harsh lessons of old mistakes
and tears of tender loss
with acceptance and courage
into a fertile foundation
for vulnerable growth.

Hi there.

Just wanting you to know, I quit work last week because my blood pressure was soaring, and I was getting a lot of tiredness from my heart thumping so hard. If this working was good for me, I know it is because I found a neat doctor. Besides being the cutest durn doc in the country, he is funnier 'n heck and he thinks I'm a good ol' gal. He's about forty-one. One day at the hospital, he was sputtering about the hospital administration board. I took the liberty to pat him on the back and tell him to "take it easy, you little firecracker. . . ." He laughed and said, "You're the mother-type, aren't you?"

After that, we always made rounds together. I made cotton doughnuts for his old patients' bedsores, and he asked me if I was a WWI nurse (eeks!). He hadn't seen any nurse do that before. Anyway, I've now got a doc I like and trust. My blood pressure is coming down with his prescription. I had an EKG run, and he will tell me results next Tuesday. My heart quit beating against my ribs, and I got my garden planted.

I now have up—peas, Swiss chard, radishes, lettuce, garlic, dry onions, three hundred strawberries, and fifty raspberry bushes. A fence is built around my veggie garden from the pipeline to the grape vineyard to keep the ducks, geese, and the chicks out. I have ten hens setting now and three turned off with babies. Chicks running nuts around here and the old mama's keeping them around in each little family. The old gray goose is setting. Redwings and robins are coming back. Quail skeeter along the road. It's a good place, and I'm happily doing OK.

Love you all—take care.

Gaga Fern

Goslings in the Reeds

Eleven fuzzy heads quiver,
hidden beneath
the tender spring reeds.
The goslings are crouched in the mud
lining the bank of the pond.

The babies nuzzle
and mutter gentle chirps,
their downy coats, not yet feathers,
glowing in the golden light
that slants across the water.

The goslings gather close with
tiny fluttering breasts—
the reeds and mud and rustling willows
their only world as they huddle
in their vulnerability.

Their wary parents stand guard,
strutting the edges of the nest,
bringing offerings of juicy grubs,
urging their brood to venture out
and forage forth.

A bright new day
shimmers upon the pond,
ripe with promise
as life begins.

My family,

This year I started to reach out to feel life with greater respect than I oftentimes have. I lay [sic] *in the hammock under the trees after I have fed the ducks, and I just float and dream for an hour feeling the glorious peace around me. This refurbishes me and remains with me while I go about taking care of activities that tax me.*

Back to my baskets! I made a dandy with that knotty yarn you and I got at the Seattle art show. Also, I made an interesting one of the bark and twigs I gathered. I am scratching designs on my gourds I grew and making paper beads from the wallpaper books I got at Christmas time. I'll enclose some here—I can decorate my baskets a little with them.

The Buhl spinners and weavers ask me if they could meet at my house for a basket-weaving lesson—so I said, proudly, of course. Supposed to be six women but turned out twelve women, one man, and two babies. I had reeds, weeds, and sticks all over the house. I had collected all the materials for them in the fall. Everyone started a basket and many finished.

There is a very exclusive shop in Ketchum that wants me to place some exceptional homemade originals. In February I will start trimming my grapevines and have now designed a basket for the grape picker—which I haven't seen one like yet. The winery here will sell them for me if they catch on popularly. I bottled my wine last week. I have six cases of nice clear Riesling wine—not too sweet.

Onward!
Love always,
Ma

Dear Family,

I hope you will get this soon as you get home because you will be wondering about me. Well, I still have the headaches. My vision isn't better and, of course, it didn't help that I backed into the garage and broke the driver's side front window. The car being an "antique," it's taking some time to find a replacement. My insurance company is going to cover it—but what a darn thing to happen!

*Anyway, since I've got those bad headaches again, I'm not going to go up to Ketchum like I planned. Don't worry about me—they'll get better—I'll just lay [*sic*] low for a bit.*

Mom

Courage

SPRING 1989

Thirteen years passed on Fern's Pond. The rhythm of the earth with all its demands and gifts brought a cadence to life unfolding; seasons lapping over seasons like the ripples on the pond. The composition of her life took shape, just as a basket might emerge. She accepted what was offered and added "something interesting"—a bit of this and an unexpected embellishment of that. Centering around a strong spine of resilience and courage, Fern lived her best life with integrity and purpose—composing her own unique story that was profound and layered.

Simply, hers.

Transition

Rolling and rocking, the rhythm of the
 train
lulls her as it sways, rolling and rocking,
 on the rails
as it carries her closer to her son and
 daughter
waiting across the mountains.

It's a sunny day in February.
Her picnic is packed—
apples and dried fruits,
homemade bread
and a wedge of cheese.
A tiny basket for her new grandchild
sits half-woven in her lap.

The train winds through the canyon,
then up the Blues to the high plateau
overlooking the boundary lands between
Idaho, Oregon, and Washington.
There the three lands of her life
converge with open arms
to carry her on to the Pacific,
into her family's embrace.

Her head rests against the seat, and she
 drifts.
She thinks softly, with pride,
of the home that is receding behind her,
of Rowdy, her dog, safe with the
 neighbors.

Soon she will return, filled
and complete.

She closes her eyes and begins to dream.
Her mother is rocking her—or is it Oscar?
Or maybe she's the one rocking
a baby in her arms—
everything will be OK.
Nodding and drifting—
everything will be OK.

Until it isn't.

Something shifts.
Something is amiss.
Deep inside, a panic rises.
She tries to make sense
as she slumps to the seat.
Her left side hangs limp.

She slides onto the floor.

The train is still rocking and swaying,
swaying and rocking, still on its way,
taking her someplace;
it's so hard to say. . . .

She tastes her panic
when she tries to speak, too frightened
for tears, her cries
are croaks. The nurse she was
knows something has broken.
Broken and lost—something stopped—
the train? It's so hard to know. . . .

On a sunny day in February
when she was seventy-five,
half of Fern's world went dark,
and her last struggle came on.

The train had carried Fern to her daughter and son in Washington State. The stroke left Fern paralyzed on her left side. After they stabilized her, she started over once again with courage. She couldn't swallow—and for a time was dependent on a feeding tube into her stomach. She couldn't move her left arm and leg and could barely speak. But inside, she remained, and, still, she wrote . . . and wrote.

Written from Rehab

*I just lay [*sic*] here and let them take care of me. I'm a trapped animal. I'm locked in, but I will get better.*

Also, I wet the bed sometimes.

Don't be sad about me. I'm going to get better. They are concerned about my body. Oh yes, but I don't want to listen. Oh, I guess I'm not too interested. I gotta discipline my thinking tho, I think about the good life I've had, and I must be as happy as I can in my condition. But the body has to recuperate as the God in heaven sees fit. I know that I gotta be positive in my thoughts about a goal. I can't get depressed!

I sure am a copout and sorry right now. But I can't make myself sick about it. I get so sad thinking about the lovely life I had and have no more. The supervisor is going to help me with an antidepressant. That may help my sadness inside. I didn't know they had so many ways to help me.

—

Isn't it nice that I can write?! It hurts my throat a little to talk much. Just the muscles and also my tummy tube. If I write, maybe I won't think.

—

It is bedtime and I can't quiet down. I'm full of stuff I wish I had time to write, but for sure I love you and have always known you love me.

Dreams

On that sunny day in February
when she was seventy-five,
half of Fern's world went dark.

Paralyzed and panicked,
she fought back.
Her brain still whole
but her body broken;
she started again
and again

to speak
to write
to eat
to walk.

But the nightmares were relentless, some
    waking,
some sleeping, her thoughts submerged
in restless dreams
tangled with regret.

She longed for home, longed
to be free. She longed and longed
to turn back the clock
to when and where her life used to be.

And always in the dream that recurred,
there was a train, and it was pushing
    words—

the same two words
up a steep and never-ending hill. . . .

Mariposa and *Marsupial*
Mariposa and *Marsupial*
Sadness and terror overwhelmed her.
Flight or dependence; resilience or
reliance.
(I will be brave.)
(I will be brave.)
And then, again,
the tears would come—

Mariposa and *Marsupial*
Butterfly or Kangaroo—the Swallowtail
dips and flickers,
beckoning. . . .

Invisible

She had become invisible.

Only the rough attention
to her constant needs,
unrelenting angst, and
gentle presence of family
connected her to the
living world.

Her soul, begging to be seen,
now cowered in fear
deep within the confines
of her diminished body
and wracked limbs.

Her terrified heart
faintly fluttered,
pulsing torment into
the shell of her former self,
yearning to be restored.

Who had she become?

Without her familiar tethers
her "self" had disappeared.
The strength and joy in her
once-vibrant life
were erased
unseen
by those who came and went
and assaulted her

dignity
with impersonal eyes.

"See me!" her tortured soul cried out.
"Hear the songs hidden and trapped
inside this useless body!

"See me. Hear me. Know me.
Pull me back to the surface
of the living—
to dwell again
among those who still offer
the essence of their whole story
intact.

"See me. See me.
Help me see myself again."

Written from Rehab

The speech therapist came to see me today and worked with me on speaking and exercising my tongue. The rest of the afternoon, I walked with the quad cane. I worked on the mat a short while just exercising my legs. I feel good, and I'm happy to work hard.

I sure had a lot of therapy yesterday—they exercised my legs and my arm. Some pain in my clavicle area on my shoulder. I exercised on a mat—my arms and legs. It is quite a workout. I got my left little finger to move. It was fun to see it jump up. My therapy gal was pleased too. They gave me a good workout. Not much swallow progress, but I have walked sixty-five feet with a quad cane.

My nurse has helped me dress, and my room is being tidied up. I hope all will be convenient for me to get my writing table. If I can write, I won't lose contact with you. I can work the puzzles, and I love to write. My friend here can swallow, but she can't write, so I feel more fortunate than she. I will learn to swallow someday.

At last, I am starting a habit to write as soon as I get up in the morning. Finally, I can swallow. I wake up early, have to potty, then sit in my chair writing until breakfast time and then go down the hall to breakfast. Later the nurse will help me dress myself.

I am content to live here in this rest home. I can come into the library and write each day. I feel like I'm doing better. I am far more fortunate than some people here. And I can write—which pleases me. I can't smile yet, tho, and I wish I could, but I can wink, and that pleases me. I can express myself a little anyway.

I go tooling around in my wheelchair and say hi to people. Sometimes they chat back. Usually, they are still eating their breakfast, tho. I like to give them a cheery "good mornin'." I think some are glad to get a cheery word from me. Maybe nobody says good morning to them. I feel sorry for some people. And I look out the windows and see birds getting their early-morning worms. I just like to look at the world out there. It's a good world.

I am finished with breakfast of cereal, boiled egg, toast, and coffee and orange juice. I ate good, but I still let drool and sometimes food fall from my mouth. I have to go slower yet, but I will learn. Maybe it will be fall of next year before I get home. I don't want people to see me drooling and say, "Oh, poor Fernie." I know with my determination, I will get better and go walking to my garden again. But I must be patient and yet work with steady confidence. I have a long journey back to what I want to do, but every day I will work with confidence in my people around me that are helping me.

To all who do not value your health now! If ever you knew what it would be like to have your beautiful spirit trapped, you would live life so beautifully every day. Once you cannot move freely *by your own power, you wonder how you ever let yourself get into such a tight corner. But I remember the good days, and so I know what to work for. I had a good youth, and I remember it as I lay [*sic*] here now. I sure do remember when I danced and rode horseback and chased the ducks.*

This is a good hospital. The supervisor is a beautiful personality. She will help me. My daughter said, think of my body with all those workers hurrying about to straighten up their home. It gave them a shock when I had a stroke! They rush about picking up each piece and placing it right where they think it needs to be—like ants in an anthill. I hope they are not like an anthill. I mean this as a joke.

Ants (2)

In Fern's dreams, the ants earnestly work
inside the labyrinth of her body
following the broken and
damaged nerves and veins.
They excavate the detritus,
repair networks,
shore up broken walls,
lay out strong highways
and smooth passages—

The ants go marching,
marching, marching
with earnest purpose,
bringing order to chaos,
rebuilding her broken body
one cell at a time.
source to home, source to home,
source to home to source again.

With endless toil,
singular focus, and supernatural strength,
they forage and haul bits of
discard—scavenging detritus
from the ravaged landscape—
building and rebuilding.
The ants go marching
one by one by one.
Step by step by step.

Written from Rehab

After you left me last night, I carefully looked at the pictures of my home. I see the rowboat and my entry porch with my big iron bell. I see the front porch of my home, and I see the barnyard. And I see the rimrocks where the eagles fly high from and float through the air. Each picture is a clear memory teaser of my good home in Idaho.

I tried to write a letter to my friends, but in reading over it, I lose some of my words—perhaps they are on my left side and I forgot to search thoroughly for them. Besides, I forget how to spell that word, "thoroughly." I shall have to be more careful and slow down in order to improve my letter writing. I must remember to write plainly and go slower. I'm too impulsive or impatient. I must go slower.

Dear Friends,

Just a quick little note to you. I have started my day here in this nice rest home rehab place. Soon I will go to have physical therapy, and hopefully I shall be able to walk a little bit more with a quad cane. My left arm is like a broken wing, but I will fly out of this coop someday and use my feet to navigate. Many people don't have use of one arm, so I won't let that stop me very much. I'll be a toughy.

Tell my neighbors I think of them often and hope they think of me as they look out their window at my place. Do you all see my ducks? I bet they have increased in number and have mated and will have young ducklings darting around my lovely pond free as birds can be and turning their white tails up in the air as they dig their beaks in to get something to eat off the pond growth. Maybe they eat the moss or maybe they eat snails off the weeds in the pond. I hope you enjoy seeing them.

I'm not as I used to be on the outside, but inside my hide I'm still me—never say quit—just keep on trying. I am learning to walk, and hopefully when I come home, I can walk down the road to my big trees and hear the redwing blackbirds sing in the cattail bushes and pause to listen if the magpies are in the tree as usual to rob some other bird's little nest. I dream of my place, so it is a heaven to me. I will see my hammock swing between the trees and remember when I sat in it looking up at the rimrock to see if I could spot an eagle flying high and free as a bird can be.

With love to you all,
Fernie

Written from Rehab

Good morning—

I just finished my breakfast, and I was told by Kate that my room will be changed. Hope everything will be transferred. I would hope my letters and pen will be put in my bedside stand where I can get to them. I want to write today.

It is now 3 p.m., and I find out it is Wednesday, the 24th of May. I had speech therapy a while ago. I walked in the hall a lot today—I am getting stronger. Here I am in my new room. I can see the hall clock, and I feel quite at home here. My OT came to see me and brought my last ceramics. There is a green frog for you to take home.

I've been worrying about trying to go home to live. I don't see how that could work out. I don't want to go back to my home for a long time yet. I want to be able to walk out on the porch before I go home. I don't want any pity. Oh gosh! This is awful hard to take!

I'm not scared anymore. I just don't want pity. I don't want to see my neighbors and have them pity me. I will float away without pain or worry if I die. There will be no more worry when the angel comes for me. I dreamed about this last nite.

I'm sorry to leave such a mess for you to have to straighten out, but I can't worry myself into another stroke over that now. My calf you can sell. Maybe the baby chicks will become tender fryers by summertime. But don't save them for me. My buggy you can sell someday. My farming days are not important to me now. From now on it is get well, get stronger, get more active. I want to be able to go down the cement steps to the little boat and then get in the boat and have someone row me around the pond.

Love to all—
Ma Fern

June 1989

I am alone in bed. My folks have gone home. Today was a good day. My family came to share Father's Day with me. We sat outside together and played a game. My grandsons were so fun—treating their old Gaga so good and teasing me too. It was all just like it used to be.

My dear,

I am so grateful as I look at the pictures of my Idaho home. I have finished with my dinner. I showed my pictures to my night nurse. I'm proud of my home. It's good to look at the pictures and remember good times there. I feel like just being happy tonight for such memories of home. It is only 5:30 and too early to go to bed. I got my toothbrush to help me get my hankie off the bar over my bed. I like to do for myself whenever I can. I like this place. I had coffee and cookies in a room with music this afternoon. They played on a mouth harp "When It's Springtime in the Rockies," and I sang to myself all the words. I have been showing my pictures to the nurses. What a wonderful good thing to show. I have run out of time and paper.

This may be my last time to write, and I want you to know I close my eyes and see your shining hair, and I am most happy for the picture I see. I love you so much, and I know you love me too. I'm hanging in there for your sake and for my sake too. Love is such a tonic of good medicine for me. And I know you love me, my dear.

Nity nite, sweetheart—Remember, I love ya,

Ma

Epilogue

SUMMER 1989

Two days later, Fern suffered another massive stroke that sent her into a deep coma. She never regained consciousness and lingered for two days before slipping peacefully free on June 22, 1989. She was courageous to the last—holding on until we assured her that it was OK to let go; that we would carry on her legacy for the next generation of grandchildren as long as we could. I sang "Summertime" to her as she gently faded away.

Flight

Moments before,
Fern had felt life's final warmth.
Cradled in the arms of her son and
    daughter,

gentle fingers caressed her brow,
brushing back the wisps of white hair
that lay flat against her cool skull,
tucking the strands behind her ears,
away from her watery blue eyes
that could no longer see.

Velvet skin, film over bone,
now as translucent as the membrane
holding the yolk of an embryo.

Her beloved used old body, once
a vessel of strength, now wracked and
    bent,
longed only to be free

while her soul waged one last futile fight.
    Torn
between staying and leaving, lingering,
she held on

with gentle fury, waiting and waiting,
    resisting, suspended in the void,
denying

the growing light, as if sheer will could
    shift the ultimate—the cleaving—
until, with final amazement, the path
    beyond was revealed
and bravely, with courage and gratitude,
she surrendered.

That moment. That exquisite, sacred
    moment.

Profile

Following the ceremony—
after the last neighbors had gone
and the people from the church had
taken the tables and chairs,
and the dishes and
afternoon naps were done—
our family assembled for the
long hike to the top of the cliff.

The still heat of that mid-July day
in the high Idaho desert
finally released its stifling grip,
exhaling a hint of a breeze.

Time to go.

We made our way, carefully, up
the gravel road to the highway,
across a sloping pasture of
brittle grass, nettles, and boulders
to the base of the lava wall.

Six hundred feet above the valley floor
our destination was etched
into the eastern rim of the valley,
where a silhouette,
perfectly formed by the outline of rocks,
showed against the horizon.

Everyone who knew her saw it—
clearly Fern's profile against the cliff.

There she reclined with a steady gaze
across the Snake River Valley—
her ample bosom forming
a lower plateau, her brow, distinctive
nose, her chin, even her hair as
tufts of sagebrush at the top.

And we felt it, her presence
watching over us
and her land.

Her valley.
Her pond.
Her home.

And now, we are taking her on one last
climb.
This time to stay
forever.

She must have known it would take
all of us at last
working together
to make it to the top
and down again.
What she could never dictate in life—
she might yet accomplish in death.

She would have teared up,
mopping her pale blue eyes
with her ever-present man's kerchief,
at the absolute rightness of the task
and her pride in her now-orphaned family,

if she'd seen us making our way
to the steep climb.

Seeking a route without a trail,
we stepped through the nettles, dry sage,
slipping shale, as we followed
the swallowtail butterfly
that circled and dipped alongside us,
guiding our way forward.

Hands reaching, pulling up, or
supporting from behind,
we avoided the sharp edges of black
    obsidian
and picked our way—
someone sometimes leading,
someone sometimes following,

belaying our sorrow up the face,

watching for snakes venturing out into the
    evening cool,
noting scat from coyotes,
a feather dropped by the nesting eagles
from the sheer rise above.
We worked against the slanting sun in the
    waning hour
to reach the top together
and deliver our precious cargo.

She would have loved the theater of it all
(except the part about being in a black
    plastic box).
Fern was never one to be carried.

She had always climbed the cliffs high
 above the valley
under her own power
to reach the perch above her brow—

to look down on the sheep wagon nestled
 in the trees,
the pond that wrapped its arms
around the sloping vineyard, the bountiful
 garden,
her sturdy log house—
to watch the smoke curl from the massive
 chimney.

Still climbing, we reminded ourselves
that despite the plastic box
she was already free—
her spirit riding the dry wind
that rolled up over her profile's chest,
against her chin and ruffled the wisps
crowning her right temple.

Finally, perched on the high cliff,
we drew around the open box
to fulfill the last wish of our mother.

*Hike up the cliff and throw my ashes off
 my nose.*
So, Fern had directed. And so, we would.

One by one we reached in
and sprinkled the white dust and bits of
 charred bone
over the edge of the cliff,

melding her remains with the profile of
rock
that reclined against the lava's edge.
Over her brow, the bridge of her nose,
and soft upon her eyes.

A brief uplift of air
rising from the valley below
seemed to signal the arrival
of a receiving soul
and carried the remaining filament
to a self-chosen
resting place
against the rocks.
As the sun settled lower,
the heavens began to fill with the glorious
colors
of a late-summer sunset in the high
prairie.
Blazing ribbons of golds and oranges,
swirls of reds and violets.
Bursts of yellows.
Pools of indigo.

The colors knew no boundaries.
Flowing from the western hills to the
eastern plateau
along the undulating valley to the south,
bordered by the snowcapped peaks in the
north.

Our celebration swelled
across the full arc of the sky
with the brilliance of farewell—

to another day, another life,
to a spirit, a force, and a gift.

The universe stretched out its glorious
    cloak
and wrapped our fragile circle
in one last embrace.
We sang her old cowboy songs,
and dusk began.

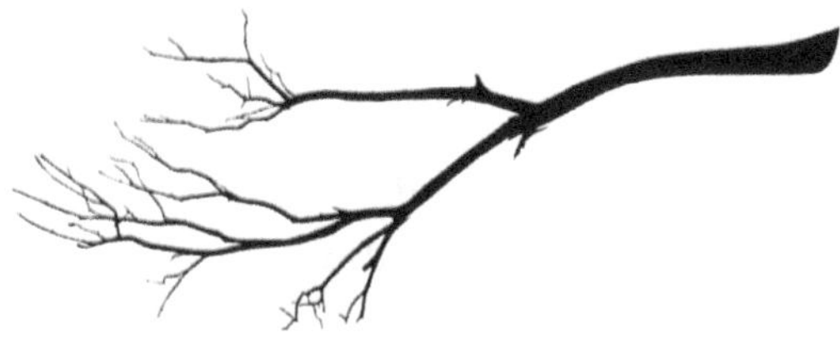

Denouement

2021

Life continued to unfold on Fern's Pond. Thirty-two years passed. Sixteen grandchildren were born, and some were lost. Her son raised his own family within the sturdy walls of the old log house. And then, he, too, passed.

But still, the home remained strong and loved by her family. We gathered for reunions, holidays, graduations, weddings, and just to be together. As Fern had dreamed, her family had found a new "home," and a new generation of memories was nurtured on Fern's Pond.

Dust to Ash

Mother's Day weekend

Before morning dawned,
the old log home blazed down.

A storm churned up from the south,
rattling the pine branches, snapping the
    one line
arcing from transformer
to roof. Lashing the dawn.

The reins of a frantic stallion
frothed in fury—
a spark. A gasp. A roar.
The tinderbox ignited

and flames seared the silent predawn sky
reflected in the pond.
A golden sunrise or rippling sunset—
the beginning or an end.

Fern's granddaughter's family
with their baby girl
fled the inferno in their nightclothes
with only what they could grab
in the hellish light.

Transfixed and traumatized with
    anguished disbelief
they fell to their knees
and watched it all burn down.

Three days later, the remainder of our
family
has gathered
to excavate our lives
and salvage what remains—
unrecognizable after the ravaging flames
and torturing heat.

We stand in stunned silence,
not knowing where to start.

Smoldering logs, tangled piano wires,
broken stained glass doors, the old brass
bed,
uniforms and dolls and baby clothes;
silks on screens, arrowheads, and stamps
and
so much more.
Generations of collections
that no one saw
now litter a tomb.

We weep as we shovel each square foot by
square foot.

Scoop. Sift. Filter. Discard.
Scoop. Sift. Filter. Discard.

Ashes of dreams unlived,
ashes of love and regret.

All afternoon we scoop.
We sift. We filter. We discard.

Only the stone hearth where we warmed
  our backs
on cold winter mornings
now offers a place to rest
and wipe our tears.

The stoic chimney still shoulders the
  center beam.
That one enormous log, the apex of the
  house,
the fulcrum of our lives,
hangs perfectly balanced and charred,
scarring the blue, cloudless sky

accusing and defying those who dwell
in heaven now, or now in hell.

December

Wild has returned to Fern's Pond, and
only the profile remains.

A biting wind cuts through the canyon,
swirling up from the Snake,
rebounding against the sheer lava cliffs,
gripping the waters below
in icy stillness.

A clear winter sky with its distant sun
has kept the temperature below twenty
    degrees
for over a week.
Ice, creeping steadily toward the
center of the pond,
remains fragile at the edges—
breaking up as three ducks nudge and
    dive,
searching for remnants to sustain them
a few more days.

The pond curls around the scarred
and barren earth and shivers
against the brown grasses lining the
    banks.
Bubbling up from the southeast corner,
an underground spring rises
from under a tight crown
of watercress, fresh water cutting a path
through the frozen surface.

Stark locust trees brace the east rim of the
pond,
their ribbed trunks slicing black lines into
the grays,
khakis, and dirty whites.
Spent cattails release their
few remaining tufts of seed
onto the frozen mud and nestle in
for the long wait until spring.

The cold has a silence broken only
by the mutterings of the ducks
and the rustle of dry branches
as the wind plays
along the banks
of Fern's Pond.

ACKNOWLEDGMENTS

I am truly grateful for those have "seen" me, loved me, encouraged me, challenged me, and inspired me to continue through the journey of creating this book. You made me believe it was possible:

Nick and Andy—always and forever
My Steve
Nancy
Tara
Annie K.
Lynda W.
Linda H.
Sally and Brad
Linda and Joel
Catherine and Dominique
Killian and Bernie
Teachers . . . and,
of course,
Fern.

Finally, special thanks to the team at Girl Friday Productions.

BOOK CLUB QUESTIONS

1. What personal connections did you make to the book or to Fern? What do you think the author was trying to say?

2. Fern longed to live her life authentically and with integrity, holding strong to her values. In what ways do you feel that she met those intentions?

3. How was Fern's skill in basketmaking a metaphor for how she lived her life?

4. How do you think who Fern became as an adult was shaped by her early life? Can you pinpoint any pivotal turning points in her development?

5. How has your life been shaped by your past? How has it been shaped by your ancestors? How are you like or unlike them?

6. In *Songs from Fern's Pond,* the land and the creatures living there are also characters in the story, and Fern generously nurtured them. How does your life nurture the other lives that surround you?

7. In the poem "Invisible," Fern longs to be "seen." What does it mean to "see" someone in all their complexities?

8. Fern lived her life with "courage, gratitude, joy," and "fearless acceptance." How do you think these values supported her resilience in meeting the challenges of her life? Are there ways you can enhance your own resilience and well-being?

9. What role did learning play in Fern's vibrant life? In what ways do you challenge yourself with continuous learning? In what areas of your life would you like to continue to grow, and what steps might you take to support this growth?

10. Fern taught that every life has obstacles and, with them, the opportunity to see oneself as either a victim or as a participant in creatively navigating a new path. Are there ways you see this playing out in your own life?

11. In what ways are you "composing" your own life to align with your passions and circumstances? Is there a role for creativity and improvisation in your life? If so, how does it manifest? If not, what steps could you take to open that door?

12. If you were sitting with Fern, what questions would you have for her?